RHYMES AND REFLECTIONS IN INK

A REPERTOIRE OF POEMS

RUPALI MISTRY

Made with ♥ on the Notion Press Platform
www.notionpress.com

This book is dedicated to my parents - Mr. Biman B. Mistry and Mrs. Roma Mistry, for always inspiring me; to my relatives, who added to my wisdom; to my friends, for the endless fun and conversations; to my country - India, whose culture runs in my veins; to Mother Earth, for being my one true abode, and to the entire Universe, for enabling my dreams to manifest.

Contents

Contents

1. Take a Pause

Take a Pause

Now, what would be a cause for a pause?
We could carry on endlessly like a clock.
More work could be accomplished daily
If there were no reasons for a dilly dally.
Just imagine a life where you don't stop
And keep on spinning like a child's top –
A series of tasks, reports, and deadlines –
More profits and improved bottom-lines.
Now, pray, come with me to the garden.
Let's walk, taking the path less trodden.
Look at the ladybugs, all red and black
On the white roses lining the dirt track.
The grass shines like Indian emeralds
As dew glistens on leaves and petals.
Listen to the symphony of the evening –
The bees humming, the birds singing.
And yonder are the dark olive-green hills
Standing stoically not unlike sentinels.
Witness the skies turn bright crimson
As they say goodbye to the setting sun.
Can you see the shapes in the clouds?
Two fiery dragons engaged in a bout.
Let's stroll on till the moon peeps out
Lighting up our way in a silver shroud.
Tomorrow will arrive at its quick pace
And its series of chores and challenges,
But wouldn't you agree that it's better
If you took a break in the lap of nature?

Rejuvenate the cogwheels of the mind,
Forgetting the deadlines for some time.
Take a long walk, and you will figure
That this pause will make you the richer.

2. Treasures of the Past

Treasures of the Past

Some say what's out of sight is out of mind,
And this is also true for the steady flow of time –
Seconds, minutes, hours, days, years and decades,
With every passing moment, they all fade away.
They take with them experiences sad and happy
And seal these in a cabinet labelled "Memories."
The cherished ones at times pop up in the mind,
But many of these are forgotten and left behind.
Oh! To catch and freeze all those moments
With the details just as they were in that instance –
The dress, shoes, eyes, garden, smile, and rapture.
Yes! All these are captured in a beautiful picture.
These images are all treasures from our pasts.
They are the ones that make the lost times last.
Be it people, places, adventures, events or things,
A photograph is sure to pull the heart's strings.
And whenever you want to relive those moments,
All you need is to look at the pictures in albums.

3. If We Ever Meet Again

If We Ever Meet Again

If we ever meet again,
I'd hold your hand and never let go
Be it blustering winds, hail or snow.
If we ever meet again,
I'd walk with you on the sandy beach
And listen to you tell me your dreams.
If we ever meet again,
I'd capture your picture with my eyes —
The way you laugh and the way you smile.
If we ever meet again,
I'd spend all of my moments with you —
Forget the past, make memories new.
If we ever meet again,
I'd tell you my secrets — my heart's truths.
And waste no time to say — I love you.

4. Summer Days

Summer Days

The sunlight bouncing off
The leaves on the trees
Leaves bright motifs on
The floor through the grills.

The whispering wind
Blowing ever so slowly
Makes every moving thing
Rejoice in joyous dancing.

The koel singing softly –
Songs floating in the breeze.
What could the notes mean?
Maybe love's sweet melody.

The sun looking handsome
Rising in the eastern skies
Frowns glaringly by noon
Like a lover tired of waiting.

The hills turning brown
With their sun burnt faces
Tell stories of their own
To anyone who listens.

The sky showing its colors
Without any cloudy specks
Is that Eternal Artist's canvas
With Art that can't be imitated.

The beautiful summer day then
Bids adieu as evening creeps
With the sun setting in the west,
Its tete-a-tete a complete mystery.

These days, these golden days
In beauty are truly unparalleled.
O sands of time – pray stop and stay!
These summer days are all I crave!

5. The Folded Page

The Folded Page

It was a strange time.
Standing at the edge,
I was unable to decide –
Should I take the step?
A lot had been advised.
A lot also introspected.
Yet I stood on the line
Fearing the unexpected.
What if I should fail?
What if I should lose?
Defeated by self-blame,
I searched for a truce.
Should I turn back?
Should I reconsider?
Maybe another plan
Could avoid failure.
Frustrated, I scribbled
"I Can't" on a blank page.
Then, left it folded,
Trying hard to forget.
With no decision yet
I unfolded the page.
The crease had split
The written phrase.
Then, it was that I saw
The "I Can" in the "I Can't."
And, with a feeling of awe
I let go of my "Shan'ts."

We all need such messages
At the crossroads of our lives.
And, this is how a folded page
Helped me overcome my strife.

6. The Girl in the Clouds

The Girl in the Clouds

She was a fleeting vision
Of translucent iridescence
As she strolled in silence
Under the colored heavens.
Grey ribbons that tamed
Her shoulder-length hair
Beautifully complemented
Her long, flowing dress.
And bell-shaped sleeves
Billowing with the breeze
Were matched by the wave
Of the sash on her waist.
Her head leaned towards
A book held in her hands;
She was totally oblivious
Of all the curious glances.
Then a gust hurried by-
She gazed up just a while,
Gave a small, courteous bow,
And suddenly, she was gone.
Merging into all the shades
Like water-drops on wet paint.
"Marvellous!" I thought aloud,
Of the girl I saw in the clouds.

7. The Journey Alone

The Journey Alone

I went on a journey alone
Down a long, winding road.
On the way, I met some flowers.
I rejoiced in seeing their colors.
A few smiled at me cheerfully
While other prickly ones hurt me.
Then, there were the great trees.
Shielding me from gusty breeze,
With sweet fruits that I could eat,
And leafy beds for me to sleep.
The road I walked had rocks in it.
On some, I stumbled down and fell
While others let me sit and rest
Giving respite to my tired legs.
As I skipped to the road's end,
I came to a mighty, blue ocean.
In it, I swam with all my strength,
Against the tides and currents.
Till I reached my final destination —
A place that was beyond description.
With no crowns or victory trophies,
Just a sense of satisfaction in me,
For this journey I took by myself
Is the bittersweet story of life itself.

8. Broken ... And Fixed

Broken ... And Fixed

It started with a fight.
We argued, shouted, sweared, and called each other names.
I stomped up to the attic.
My face flushed and teary-eyed in a fit of rage.
I somehow had to end this.
The only way to save myself was to consciously separate.
This relationship that I cherished,
A year later, had become stale.
Just then, my eyes fell on a wooden chest.
It was an old one made of wood and nails.
I mindlessly opened it,
Rummaging through the bric-a-brac it contained.
Suddenly, I found myself holding my dolly.
She was small, with a blue dress and a pink face.
Her arms were covered by bell sleeves,
But they were held to her body with tape.
There was an inundation of memories.
Decades ago, my friend and I were engrossed in play.
This dolly was one of my favorites,
And when we both grabbed it together, her arms gave way.
We tried to play with her.
But then decided it was useless and to throw her away.
Just then, my grandmother walked in.
She took one look at the dolly and shook her head.
With scissors, tape, and, in fifteen minutes,
My little dolly was ready to play with again.
"When something is broken, look for ways to fix it."
Her words echoed in my mind at that very moment.

All of a sudden, I felt like a bulb had been lit.
Yes, there was anger, frustration, and rage,
But, I was going to try and save this relationship
I walked out of the attic, ready to calmly explain what I felt.

9. The Wager

The Wager

'Twas the summer season
In the great Indian plains.
The heat was unforgiving
In every town and village.
On one such lazy afternoon
In the village of Nenaanoo,
Little Jon and his pals, too
Wondered what to do.
It was too hot to play ball
Or Chupa chupi or Pithoo
Or Gilli Danda or Kho kho
Or Five Stones or Lattoo.
Soon, they started arguing
About who was more clever.
And in the heat of the moment,
The lads agreed to a wager.
The target was a mango tree
Owned by the uppity Mr. Wick.
It was guarded by ol' Kenie
Who carried a wooden stick.
The tree was heavily laden
With mangoes ripe and golden
Whoever picked five of them
Would be the cleverest one.
And so they crept to the tree.
In silence, the race began.
They heard ol' Kenie snoring
And soon climbed up a branch.

But ol' Kenie wasn't asleep,
He woke up with a loud snort.
And he started chasing them,
So the plan they had to abort.
Down the tree, they all leapt
And scrambled to run away.
But they all stumbled and fell,
As they got in each other's way.
And so it was as the Sun set,
They returned black and blue.
For ol' Kenie had caught them
And given them a thrashing, too.
That's how the story ended
Of Little Jon and his friends.
They never laid a wager again
In the heat of the moment.

10. To the Butterfly

To the Butterfly

O beautiful butterfly
Flitting in the bower,
You shimmer vibrantly
In the bright sunlight
Among all the flowers!
Do you ever notice
The myriad colors
Splashed gleamingly
On your little wings
As you airily flutter?
Some say you're blind
To your own beauty;
The shades that shine
As you fly and alight,
You'll never know or see.
But I differently opine,
For if that were true
How could you ever find
Another one of your kind,
Just as beauteous as you?

11. Hope - A Story

Hope - A Story

The train started from a tiny village
Deep within the Indian hinterland.
And, in one red and black carriage
Sat Ami with a brown bag in her hand.
The train was bound for the big city.
The journey was of a night and day.
Soon, the whistle blew, and it slowly
Moved with a chug-chug on its way.
Along with Ami in the compartment
Were a bunch of old men and women.
She did not have to give any explanation.
They could see that she was pregnant.
The women smiled and gently asked
Her about her family and her baby.
In casual conversation, the time passed.
Then night fell, and they all went to sleep.
Sometime before dawn, Ami awakened.
The pain had started like ocean waves.
Her wails woke up the men and women.
They realized the baby was on its way.
The news spread throughout the cabins
As the women rallied around her to help.
Water, towels, bedsheets, and curtains
Were all arranged around her small bed.
After hours of the painful contractions,
Ami delivered a beautiful, pink baby girl.
Everyone wished her with congratulations
As she kept weeping with joyful tears.

Slowly, she revealed her life's story.
Her husband was martyred recently.
All that was left of his love was the baby
Whom she named "Hope" in his memory.

12. The Flower and the Stone

The Flower and the Stone

The flower bloomed high up on the tree.
A splash of red among the green leaves.
The stone sat on the cold earth's floor —
Midnight-black, and in a constant stupor.
Contented, they were, in their own worlds
Oblivious to how their fates would unfold.
The fragrant flower smiled in the breeze
While the stone stood unmoving, stoically.
One day, the rain fell from the grey skies.
Along with it, a gust of wind passed by.
The delicate flower was soon detached,
And it floated down from the tree's lap.
It twirled away in its freedom newfound
Landing at the stone's foot on the ground.
In that fortuitous moment of Pushpanjali,
The impassive dark stone attained Divinity.

13. Who Am I?

Who Am I?

I am in the beat of a heart that yearns.
I am in the pain during a child's birth.
I am in the old leaf falling from a tree.
I am in the prayer riding on the breeze.
I am in the silence that ends the fight.
I am in the wrong done to make it right.
I am in the eyes that light up with smiles.
I am in the memories that haunt at night.
I am in the hand that gives more than asked.
I am in the sweat that completes each task.
I am in the snuggles on a grey, rainy day.
I am in the cheer that's shouted on the way.
Who am I? I hide; I am hidden; I seek,
I am sought; I reveal and I am revealed.
Forever, like the precious treasure trove,
I am the reason for it all – I am love.

14. My Bed

My Bed

I cannot deny it – I love my bed.
It's more than just a place where I rest.
Though there's a desk, chair, and closet,
In my room, my bed is my favorite.
It's my philosopher and guide
And teaches me a lot about life.
Enclosed in its coziness, I sleep at night –
A sleep that helps recharge my mind.
And what I learn from it is that
When the day has been frustratingly bad,
A deep sleep will untangle the threads
And give me strength for the next day.
My bed is where I see dreams.
It's where I battle nightmares.
And it's also the place I say thanks
When my eyes open to another day.
And in the morning, when I'm awake,
My bed is the first thing I make.
For, I can't predict the course of the day,
But, at its end, I know I'll have a good rest.
My bed is my best friend.
It's not just a piece of wood.
It's more than just a place where I rest.
I cannot deny it – I love my bed.

15. It's a Girl!

It's a Girl!

"It's a girl!" they told the mother
Who gazed with love filled eyes
Upon her little daughter
For the very first time.
"It's a girl!" they told the father
Whose heart swelled with pride
As he promised to be her
Best friend and her guide.
"It's a girl!" they told the grandma
Who smiled so happily
At the thought of having someone
To listen to her stories.
"It's a girl!" they told the grandpa
Who got up and danced
As he held his granddaughter
So lightly in his arms.
"It's a girl!" they told her brother
Who clapped his hands with joy
As now he had a sister to
Play with and share his toys.
"It's a girl!" said the Wise One
As He smiled at them from above.
"She was made by all the angels
With things lovely, sweet and pure."
It's a girl! It's a girl!
As she steps into the world
With a special purpose,
She should be nurtured

With kindness and love
And a whole lot of care as
She deserves the chance to
Live, be happy and prosper.

16. Little White Roses

Little White Roses

Little white roses
Growing by the road.
Little white roses
With hearts made of gold.
Little white roses
Though they cannot speak,
Say much more than anyone
With feelings twice as sweet.
Little white roses
Spreading love and peace.
Innocent white roses
Never causing grief.
Little white roses
Give the fragrance of life.
O erring, hurting humans!
May they be your guide.

17. On Happiness

On Happiness

So, since when did happiness become a problem?
Didn't God make all of us in a likeness of His own?
We spent millions searching for a gene or chromosome,
And describing all the neurotransmitters in tomes.
Did we find the secret to everlasting contentment?
A pill, powder, or syrup to eliminate all resentment?
Could we capture exuberance in a little bottle
For a shot of exhilaration to put life in full throttle?
Why did it take us centuries to finally realize
How happiness can be manifested in our lives?
That, at times, we need to stop spinning on our axes
And seek within ourselves a state of pure bliss.
A touch, a melody, a fragrance, a taste, a picture
That revives a memory or creates a feeling of rapture.
Being thankful for all that was, is, and yet to come.
And giving away things to those who have none.
Not all of us were born with a silver spoon,
But we all have what it takes to be happy as a boon.
Just like a basket is spoilt by one rotten apple,
A smile easily spreads the jollity virus in people.
Light is best appreciated when there is darkness.
Just so, life is balanced by cheerfulness and sadness.
And if you need guidance, take a look at the little ones.
So, since when did happiness become a problem?

18. Incomplete

Incomplete

I have wings,
But without the flowing winds,
I am incomplete.
I have eyes,
But without the glowing light,
I am incomplete.
I have a mind,
But without the Divine guide,
I am incomplete.
I have a heart,
But without a true-blue confidant,
I am incomplete.
I have words,
But without a quill and paper,
I am incomplete.
It would seem,
That I am incomplete
Without the world around me.
Could it also be that the world
Is a bazillion-piece puzzle
That's incomplete without me?

19. An Auto Ride

An Auto Ride

The hands of the clock move to five,
It's time for me to get out of the hive.
I rush downstairs to the parking lots
For a ride home in the autorickshaw
The meter's down; we're on our way.
And on the road, there's a lot of traffic.
With a loud honk, a red bus passes by:
The auto swerves – missing a motorbike.
It bumpity bumps over all the potholes
Like the little cars at a car-racing show.
Now on the highway, it picks up speed
And I wobble like jelly on the back seat.
Up and down the bridges, we roller coast,
Moving in a sea of loud beeps and honks.
O what a ride! What a thrilling ride it is!
In the little auto on the city's big streets.
Here comes the house and then it ends.
The meter stops and the fare is paid.
Butterflies and prayers are laid to rest as
I look forward to the ride on another day.

20. Dear Silence

Dear Silence

Dear Silence,
Thank you for just showing up and being there.
Without you, there would be cacophony everywhere.
And with you, the noise makes sense.
Dear Silence,
Your value is beyond measure.
Just like pearls are discovered in an ocean by a diver,
The mind uncovers wisdom in your presence.
Dear Silence,
It's paradoxical, but you are an excellent orator.
Of things left unsaid, you are the messenger,
And you have salvaged many-a-worsening situation.
Dear Silence,
I appreciate you being such a life-saver.
Serenity abounds with you as the mediator.
Thank you for creating the perfect balance.

21. What's in My Name?

What's in My Name?

What's in my name? It was never mine.
Although I'll bear it for my entire life.
No, I had neither choice nor any say
In the name I'm called with every day.
So what's in my name, you would say?
Call me differently, and I'll be the same.
But when I think about it, I do realize
That my name was never really mine.
It was what my family envisioned for me
When I arrived – their hopes and dreams.
In that name, they felt all the happiness.
That name resounded with my existence.
With this name, I will never feel lonely
For I'll carry with me a piece of my family.
The name I bear may not be my definition
But behind it lie the purest intentions.
So what's in my name? Well, it's clear –
It's a sign by my ancestors, my dears.
It was never for me to use by myself.
It's not a description, but my inheritance.

22. Storms

Storms

Storms reveal
The power to heal.
The moment of birth,
The moment of death,
The events between
Are all stormy.
Storms create
The strength to adapt.
All of life's changes,
The resistance and plunges,
That define and redefine,
Are all stormy.
Storms reveal
The ability to resile.
All the challenges
That shake or break,
Leading to a rebounding,
Are all stormy.
From every storm
Arises a new form.
It's a chance to clean
The slate and start again
With endless possibilities
And probabilities.

23. Peace

Peace

It takes just one spark of anger
To set hearts ablaze with hatred
Leading to bloodshed and war,
Mindless destruction and death.
The dead cannot love or hate.
That's the prerogative of the living.
Of what use are the dead anyway?
Life is only for the alive and kicking.
The need of the hour is peace
To save Humanity from extinction.
Let peace reside in every heartbeat,
Every family, every city, every nation.
Let it fall like raindrops from the skies
Dousing the flames of bitterness.
Let's give up all resentment and unite
To create a happy world for generations.

24. Rain

Rain

Rain – falling from the heavens
Cleansing everything
From the tallest skyscrapers
To the smallest blade of grass.
Rain – kisses from the skies
Bringing forth life
From the tiny caterpillar
To trees covered with flowers.
Rain – each drop is an emotion
Forming rivers and oceans
Like cut and leaking veins
Without cauterization.
Rain – arrows of the purest love
Shot from Cupid's bow
Arching across the firmament
With its seven colours blazing.
Rain – constantly chattering
Like a garrulous old woman
Reminiscing her stories
Of the times gone by.
Rain – woven into words
By the imagination of a poet.
A covenant from our Creator,
Rain – Rain on me forever.

25. I'm a Woman

I'm a Woman

I'm the morning mist veiling the green hills.
I'm the silvery dew dazzling on rose petals.
I'm the raindrops creating rainbows in the skies.
I'm the still lake reflecting bits of sunshine.
I'm the tidal wave crashing on sandy shores.
I'm the flashflood uprooting the earth's floor.
I'm the hurricane sweeping everything in my way.
I'm the hailstorm destroying cities in a day.
I'm the drizzle bringing forth trees from seeds.
I'm the river giving all souls the final release
I'm the delta spawning civilizations that bred.
I'm the ocean churning up both life and death.
I'm not limited by my shape or the path I make.
I'm not limited by my color or the form I take.
I'm pure, I'm sacred, I'm the incarnation of strength.
I'm gentle, I'm powerful, I'm water – I'm a woman.

26. The Awakening

The Awakening

When the Sun rises in the skies,
And spreads around its rosy light,
Sleep vanishes with the night,
For a brand new day has arrived.
As I wake up and open my eyes,
I hear the birds singing outside.
The house is peaceful and quiet.
It mirrors the peace in my mind.
The window reveals a pretty sight.
Trees glitter like emeralds bright.
Birds dart about as they take flight.
The flowers bloom on the roadside.
And before the world comes alive,
And turns on its rollercoaster ride,
I say a prayer of thanks for this life.
I'm ready to take it all in my stride.

27. The Angel

The Angel

I asked if she
Would help me
To cross the street.
My vision's a blur;
I don't even hear
My bones as they creak.
The street's so wide;
I cannot decide
Where to point my feet.
She took my hand
And like a lamb
I followed silently.
She left me standing
At the gate, wond'ring,
Of this castle by the street.
"This is where you'll be."
She said to me
And turned away to leave.
I asked her name
And why she came
And where she had brought me.
"Your angel," she said.
"And Heaven's this place
Where you'll rest in peace."

28. In the End

In the End

Beyond a certain measure,
What worth are your treasures?
Beyond a certain need,
Your desires turn into greed.
Could you ever see the colors
Of the souls that left unfettered?
Or know their race, country, religion,
Food, clothes, houses they lived in?
And if seeing is really believing,
Then all these would mean nothing,
For red is the blood in our veins,
And the air we breathe is the same.
The Maker did not discriminate
Or create the boundaries of hate.
These were invented by a few who
Never cared for the common good.
The results have always been dire,
Forcing us deeper into a dark mire.
'Til we realize the need to change –
A step at a time; it's not too late.
For in the end, all that matters is
How much you loved, laughed and lived.
For in the end, we'll lie side by side
Like grains of sand, and blades of grass.

29. The Road Itself

The Road Itself

As we journey through our lives,
What stays with us is the road we tread.
Be it through pleasant or harsh climes,
The road unravels with every step.
At times, smooth, and at times, cobbled,
At times, dusty, and at times, cracked,
At times, gravelled, and at times, potholed,
The road goes on as a never-ending track.
Sometimes, it takes us down a blind alley.
Sometimes, it descends into a valley.
Or, curve till it reaches the mountain peak,
But the road we take is our choice totally.
The road is there, it always existed.
Waiting to be walked on and discovered,
Waiting to lead to new places and people,
The road unites with the one who travels.
Countless destinations are reached
All because of the roads people take.
Yet, we do not appreciate or notice
How life intersects with the road itself.

30. The Journey of a Poem

The Journey of a Poem

It begins with an inspiration,
A fleeting thought
Speeding through the mind,
And then its caught.
The idea scribbled on paper,
Then crushed and trashed.
Slowly, it starts to shape up
In the second draft.
The words play together
To build the narrative –
A simile here; or a metaphor,
Create a bit of imagery.
The verses start forming
With meter and rhyme.
After writing and rewriting,
Flow the chiseled lines.
Here comes the final version.
And with an artsy flair,
It is released from seclusion,
Ready to be shared.
Such is the evolution
Of a work of poetry
A journey from evanescence
To a joyful reality.

31. So Say the Skies

So Say the Skies

A message from the skies
Waits to be deciphered.
A voice like yours and mine
That floats in the zephyrs.
Would the heavens ever split
Along the edges and borders
Of all the hues and tints
Spread on its vast canvas?
Would it stop giving way
To the things that can fly,
And would it discriminate
Based on a certain type?
Then, why are we divided
By these very boundaries
That give rise to hatred,
And destroy all peace?
United – we stay together
And win against all odds.
The word is loud and clear
From the blue yonder to all.

32. The Ocean

The Ocean

The ocean is deep and vast.
Its beauty is unsurpassed.
Loved by everyone, feared by all,
A treasure house it is called.
Crowned by silvery, glistening waves,
Adorned with pearls of all types,
Its colossal womb gave birth to life,
The tiny cell that bore mankind.
Forever creating and destroying,
It itself is indestructible,
Unpredictable, unconquerable,
A turbulent, tempestuous cradle.
It is a witness, undoubtedly,
Of revolutions that made history
With secrets locked in its recesses,
And many of the world's mysteries.
From time immemorial it remained
And will remain as it remained.
Revered and honoured by each one,
Be it bird, beast, or man.

33. A Saree Tale

A Saree Tale

What if a saree could speak?
What tales would it narrate?
Be it cotton, satin, or pure silk,
Is it more than just a drape?
Yesterday was just another day
When I pulled out a pink saree.
It was a beautiful, floral georgette,
And as I wore it, it spoke to me.
The first yard promised secrecy,
As it always remains hidden.
Like some aspects of me
Stay undisclosed and unseen.
The second yard promised beauty
With its colors and pretty motifs.
Like all of my unique qualities
Come together to make me me.
The third yard promised change
As I folded it into wavy pleats.
Like my moods, never the same,
Are united in my personality.
The fourth yard promised grace
As it gently curved behind.
Like the manner in which I face
All that's doled to me by life.
The fifth yard promised strength
As I drew it in front and higher.
Like my determination and grit
Through tough times, get me over.

The sixth yard promised freedom
As it draped over my shoulder.
Like my thoughts and expressions
Give me higher powers.
When I finally looked at myself,
I was overcome with happiness.
Yes, my saree was more than a dress.
My saree turned me into a Goddess!

34. Action Required - Acceptance

Action Required - Acceptance

Let's consider some perspectives.
The Sun moves around the center of the galaxy
Completing one orbit in a cosmic year.
Each cosmic year equals 230 million Earth years.
And the Sun has seen 20.5 cosmic years.
The Earth moves around the blazing Sun.
Completing one orbit in a year.
Each year equals 365 Earth days.
And the Earth has seen 4.5 billion years.
And then there's you, racing around all your desires.
Letting unfulfilled expectations rule.
Passing judgements based on emotions.
Creating definitions from perceptions.
In an average life span of seventy years,
You forget that all that matters is
Not the next day, hour or minute,
But just the next second
When you – breathe.

35. Traditional, Yet Contemporary

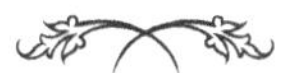

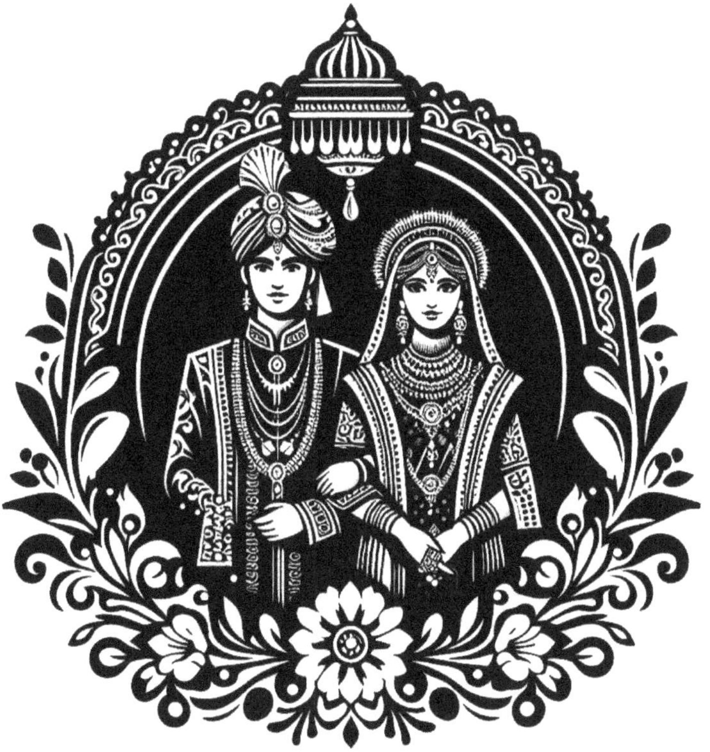

Traditional, Yet Contemporary

Wise men say – old is gold, and they say it with reason,
Like this lesson from yore, from a Hindu marriage tradition.
In one of the ceremonies, the groom shows the bride,
The twin stars, Arundhati and Vasishta, shining in the sky.
This calls upon the couple to be synced in everything,
For they are now equals, like the twin stars twinkling.
The secret to this tradition was later uncovered by scientists.
In most twin stars, one is still, and the other rotates around it.
But, Arundhati and Vasishta are unique twin stars
As they both rotate in perfect synchrony around each other.
This tells the bride and groom that to be ideal together,
Neither should feel the need to dance to the tune of the other.
How did the sages of those ancient times without modern equipment
Know about this difference of this particular star system?
Traditions are like that – mysterious yet moving us to action.
In fact, I'm sure that you all would agree with me, friends.
Anything contemporary that withstands the test of time,
Ultimately, gets transformed into a lasting and intriguing tradition.

36. Like, Comment, Share ... Despair!

Like, Comment, Share ... Despair!

Doctors of the world, beware!
A new virus is in the air!
It catches people unawares.
And spreads quickly with a scare!
The symptoms are most peculiar!
Glued to the mobile or computer,
After posting a message or picture,
The infected seek likes, comments, and shares!
It would be great if it ended there,
But every second there is to spare
Turns into this monstrous nightmare
Of wanting more likes, comments and shares!
The only thing that they care
About is how their trends compare.
Their reel life has them ensnared,
And, this leads to a lot of despair.
Now, I won't hesitate to declare
I'm caught in this trap like a hare!
And in dire need of some medicare
For my own wellbeing and welfare!
But, before I can lay my heart bare
To the doctor about this deplorable affair,
He refers me to X for his post uploaded there,
And tells me to read, like, comment, and share!

37. The Past's Perfect Memories

The Past's Perfect Memories

"He was your great grandfather,"
My grandmother said matter-of-factly.
I took a second look at the photograph
Among the many scattered around me.
I looked at the dark-skinned old man
Dressed in a white turban and dhoti.
"He was a farmer," my grandma went on,
"And he was an expert with the sarangi."
"Yes, that's correct," my father added.
"As a child, I used to sit on his shoulders
And listen to the melodies he played."
I was intrigued by the man in the picture.
The ancient photo was black and white.
Even then, I could see it was very sunny.
So many questions arose in my mind
About this stranger from my family.
What was he like? He seemed nice.
What was a sarangi? I wanted to listen.
What did he grow in the fields? Rice?
My curiosity piqued in that instant.
"Put it back carefully," my grandma said,
As I returned it into the old red album.
But, just before she turned to a new page,
I looked at my great grandfather again.
And I noticed his eyes in that picture.
He was gazing straight at me, it seemed.
I saw the affinity that was in his nature,
And, to date, I can also see that in me.

38. When Imagination Takes Flight

When Imagination Takes Flight

Logic says the Moon is far away from Earth.
384,400 kilometers away to be precise.
A thin layer of gases form its atmosphere
And breathing these would surely cause a human to die.
Its surface is uneven with many round craters
Where space rocks crash and the ground gets pulverized.
But the wings of my dreams take me on an adventure
In which I can whoosh away to the silver satellite,
And discover that it is entirely made of cheddar
As the old man living there greets me with a high five.
"But this defies logic!!!" So will say the naysayers.
And yes, it's true, what they say is right.
But listen closely to me, my brothers and sisters.
Nothing's impossible when imagination takes flight.

39. Where the Earth Meets the Sky

Where the Earth Meets the Sky

The meeting of the Earth and sky
Is but a mirage to the eye.
It is Nature's whitest lie-
A beautiful limitation of human sight.
The meeting of the Earth and sky
Is the furthest point seen in light.
Were I to try and chase this line,
Then, around the Earth, I'd take a ride.
The meeting of the Earth and sky
Is the brink of my knowledge, or might.
With experiences of a newer kind,
I can push the boundaries of my mind.
The meeting of the Earth and sky
Is also the edge of where I am in life.
It may be difficult to get to the far side,
But the possibility beckons all the time.

40. The Child in Me

The Child in Me

O! To be young again
And revisit those golden days
When I used to laugh and play
With other children of my age.
O! I recall the meadows green,
The daisies and frangipani trees.
And the many evenings that ended
By bringing home little bouquets.
O! I remember the songs I sang
Through the lyrics I didn't understand.
No matter how many times I listened
To the tape recorder with the cassette.
O! I yearn for those moments
When everything was so amazing,
And I had so many questions
Answered in books and conversations.
But as I ponder in wonder,
The thought to me does occur
That my age is just a state of my mind,
And I can rebuild what was left behind.
Why?! How lovely it would be
If I rediscovered the child in me.
If she broke through the worldly norms
Although people say she has grown up.
To be happy without restraints.
To marvel and discover in wonderment.
To retrace the footsteps of innocence.
To relive those memories in the present.

41. On Monotony

On Monotony

Of what use is monotony in life
With its tedious repetition and routine?
Is it worthless like a long drive
On a highway with scenery unchanging?
Well, if you take a microscopic view,
Monotony exists in our DNA molecules.
With mind-boggling details, these repeat
In every cell that, in a person, constitutes.
And if you look at it macroscopically,
There's monotony in the ocean waves.
Wave upon wave rises up and retreats
With every wave created just the same.
Yes, monotony is also Nature's creation,
Less valued and even less understood.
It has benefits that deserve attention.
Following a routine does a lot of good.
So, the next time you feel overwhelmed
By tasks and activities you have to do,
Know that if you follow a set routine
You can focus on what matters to you.
And, it may seem very contradictory,
But monotony will boost your creativity.
With fewer decisions to take in a day,
New ideas are generated by your brain.
So, if you want to be immune to it,
Know that it can be your best friend.
It's like the magical lamp with the genie,
But it can grant your wishes with no end.

42. Doors

Doors

Nia sat alone in her room.
With the curtains drawn, shrouded in gloom.
Her mother slowly knocked at the door.
Then, entered it to find her sitting on the floor.
On seeing her mother, Nia started crying,
"Why, mom? Why? After all this trying?"
Tears ran down her big brown eyes.
As her mother sat near her and sighed.
Holding Nia's hand, she gently spoke,
"When one door closes, another will open."
"Really?!" Nia screamed incredulously.
"Why was this door open if it wasn't meant for me?
And if the next one is indeed the one, what's that guarantee?
It's just hopeless!!" she continued tearfully.
"Nia," said her mother, "Listen to me carefully.
Each door that opens has behind it a sea of possibilities,
And every door that closes leaves us with some learnings.
When a new door opens, those turn into experiences,
Which are guiding stars as we navigate unknown oceans.
Add hard work and determination, and you'll reach your destination.
All you need to do is reassess your priorities and abilities,
And seek to improve in the areas that need it.
So, let's see what you could do better for this examination,
And let's also keep our minds open to other career options."
Having said that, she drew open the heavy curtains.
As sunshine entered the room and brightened everything,
Nia wiped her face and got up from the cold floor.
She felt ready for whatever lay beyond the next open door.

Other Publications By Rupali Mistry

Into the Kaleidoscope of Verses: A Repertoire of Poems

www.ingramcontent.com/pod-product-compliance
Lightning Source LLC
Chambersburg PA
CBHW040823120726
48005CB00012B/1489